Grandma's House

Come, Pam. Come.
Look! The bus is here.
We are going in the bus with Mummy.
We are going to Grandma's house.

PH Revise medial vowel **u**, as in **us**, **bus** and **Mummy**. **LP** Introduce question and answer drill with emphasis on the present continuous tense, e.g., *Teacher*: Where are they going? They are going to Grandma's house. *Pupils*: They are going to Grandma's house. *Teacher*: How are they going? *Pupils*: They are going in the bus. *Teacher*: Who are going? And so on. **C** Are the children going for a long visit? Who do you think is waving from the porch?

Hello, Colin. Hello, Pam.
Hi, Grandma!
Grandma's house is an old house.
Grandma's house is a pretty house.
We are going to play in Grandma's house.

PH Practise **h** as in **Hi, house, hat**. **LP** Start with a sentence from the page, e.g., *Teacher*: Grandma's house is an old house. *Pupils*: Grandma's house is an old house. *Teacher*: hat *Pupils*: Grandma's hat is an old hat. Use **chair, gate, tree, clock, vase, photograph**, etc., to continue drill. **C** Where is Mummy? Is she visiting Grandma too? Do you think the children enjoy going to see Grandma? How do you know?

We are playing in Grandma's house.
We are playing in Grandma's chair.
Grandma's chair is an old chair.
Grandma's chair is a big, soft chair.

PH Introduce **ch** as in **chair**. Pupils give other examples, e.g., **chalk**, **church**, **child**. **WA** Use flashcards with **go**, **play** and word part **-ing** to make **going** and **playing** (pp. 1–3). Use flashcards with **look**, **eat**, **jump** to make **looking**, **eating**, **jumping**. Pupils draw pictures of people and animals **looking** (e.g., in and out of windows), **eating** and **jumping**, and pin them up under the appropriate word. **C** What do you think Grandma would say if she saw Colin and Pam?

Grandma's bed is a big, soft bed.
We are playing in Grandma's bed.
Stop, Colin! Stop, Pam! Do not jump on the bed!

4 **C** Before pupils read the page, let pupils talk about the look on Grandma's face. What will she say or do? **PH** Revise final **t** as in **soft**, **not** (p. 4) and **let** (p. 5). Revise medial vowel **e** as in **bed** (p. 4) and **let** (p. 5). Talk about medial **e** in words in Twister 1. Practise saying it. Find the two word families in Twister 1. **C** What do you think about Colin and Pam playing in Grandma's bed? **A** Pupils use words in the twister to write their own poems.

Look at this jug, Colin.
Grandma's jug is an old jug.
It is a pretty jug.

Let us play with Grandma's jug, Pam.

PH Revise medial **u** as in **jug**. **WA** Use word part **-ug** to build word family **jug**, **rug**, **mug**, etc. Talk about initial consonant blend **pr** as in **pretty**. What other words do pupils know beginning with **pr** sound? E.g., **pram, pray, prince, princess, prune**. **LP** *Teacher*: This jug is mine. *Pupils*: This jug is mine. *Teacher*: This mug is mine. *Pupils*: This mug is mine. Use **rug, bed, basin**, etc., to continue drill.

Stop, Colin! Stop, Pam!
That is an old jug.
You must not play with it.

Sit on a chair, Colin!
Sit on a chair, Pam!

PH Revise **o** sound as in **stop**, **Colin** and **not** (in **cannot**). Practise **o** in Twister 2. Pupils find and sound all words with **o** as in **stop**. **LP** *Teacher: Sit on a chair, Colin. Colin is sitting on a chair. Pupils: Colin is sitting on a chair. Teacher: Stand in the corner, Pat. Pupils: Pat is standing in the corner. Continue drill, giving instructions to individual pupils. Pupils do as they are told. The class say what each is doing.* **C** Why is Grandma cross? Should she be cross?

We are sad, Grandma.
We are sorry, Grandma.
Can we get up?
Can we get up soon?

WA Use flashcard to introduce **sorry** as a sight word. PH Introduce initial consonant blend **gr**. Which group can find the most **gr** words? Practise **gr** in Twister 3. LP Use drill to practise We are. *Teacher*: We are sad. *Pupils*: We are sad. *Teacher*: Happy. *Pupils*: We are happy. Use **sorry, glad, thirsty, excited, fine, cold**, etc. to continue drill. Drill question form, Are we sad? Pupils mime looking happy, sad, etc. C Do you think the children are sorry?

Yes, you may get up now.
Come, let us sit and eat.
We are going to eat some fish.
Do you want to eat some fish?

Yes, thank you, Grandma.
We like to eat fish.
Yes, thank you, Grandma.

PH Revise final **t** as in **let**, **sit**, **eat**. Introduce initial **y** sound as in **yes** and **you**. Practise **y** in Twister 4. **LP** *Teacher*: We are going to eat fish. *Pupils*: We are going to eat fish. *Teacher*: yam *Pupils*: We are going to eat yam. Use **meat**, **breadfruit**, **roti**, etc., to continue drill. **C** How are the children feeling now? Is Grandma still upset? How can you tell? Do you think Grandma still loves them?

Grandma's clock is an old clock.
Grandma's clock is a big clock.
Bong! Bong! Bong! Bong! Bong!
We have to go.

Thank you, Grandma.
Thank you, Grandma.

Colin's Kite

Come with me to get my kite, Eric.
I am going to fix my kite and fly it.
I like to fly my kite.
My kite will be king of all the kites.

PH Introduce initial **k** sound as in **kite**. Talk about other words like **king**, **kiss**, **key**. Point out that **k** is like hard **c**.
LP Introduce a question and answer drill with pupils replying individually, e.g., *Teacher*: Where will Colin fly his kite? *Pupils*: Colin will fly his kite in the park. Teacher uses other cues such as When? Why? With whom? For how long? etc. Encourage pupils to use their imagination when responding.

I cannot find my kite.
It is a nice, big kite.
It is not on the table.
It is not on the chair.

Help me look for it, Andy.

I cannot find my kite.
It is a red and green kite.
It is not in the cupboard.
Please help me find it, Eric.
I want to fix it and fly it.

PH Introduce **x** sound as in **fix**. Practise **x** in Twister 6. Revise **f** as in **fix** and **fly**. **WA** Look at the words **cupboard** and **cannot**. Point out that they are made up of two words. How many other words do pupils know that can be split in two? Start a list. Put it up in the classroom. **C** Look in the cupboard. What can you see? Whose cupboard space is it? How can you tell? What do you think is in the other side of the cupboard?

My kite is not under the bed.
Do you see my kite, Pam?
Do you see it, Amrita?
It is a big kite and it is red and green.
Please help me find it.

PH Introduce ee sound as in **see** and **green**. Use Twister 7 to practise the sound. Revise **x** as in **fix** (pp. 10 and 12) and **box** (p. 14). Use Twisters 2 and 6 to practise **x**. Revise **f** as in **fix** and **fly**; **d** as in **bed, red, do**. **N** How many children are there in the picture? How many green and red objects are there in the classroom? **C** Why can't Colin find the kite? Do you think Pam knows where it is?

Where is my kite?
It is not on the table.
It is not in the cupboard.
It is not under the bed.

Where is it? Where is it?
Is it in the box outside?

PH Introduce initial **wh** sound as in **where**. Revise **b** as in **bed** and **box**; final **t** as in **not**, **it**, **mat** (pp. 14 and 15). Pupils give other words with final **t**. **LP** *Teacher*: Where is my kite? My kite is on the mat. *Pupils*: My kite is on the mat. *Teacher*: your *Pupils*: Your kite is on the mat. Use **his**, **her**, **our**, **their** as cues to continue drill. Revise **in**, **on**, **under**, **beside**, using objects from illustration. **C** Why do you think Pam and Amrita are whispering?

Look, Colin!
Here it is.

The mat is red and green.
The kite is red and green.
The kite is on the mat.

Thank you, Pam and Amrita.
I will fix my kite and fly it.
My kite will be king.

PH Revise initial **k** sound as in **kite** and **king**. Help pupils find final **k** (p. 15) as in **look** and **thank**. Revise **gr** blend as in **green**, **grape**, **grass**, etc. Practise Twister 8. Divide class into groups. Which group can think of the most **gr** words? Revise **x** as in **box** (p. 14) and **fix**. Practise Twisters 2 and 6. **C** Why do you think Colin says his kite will be king? What does he need to fix on his kite? **A** Talk about kites. Work in groups. Have pupils make a simple kite.

Simon Says

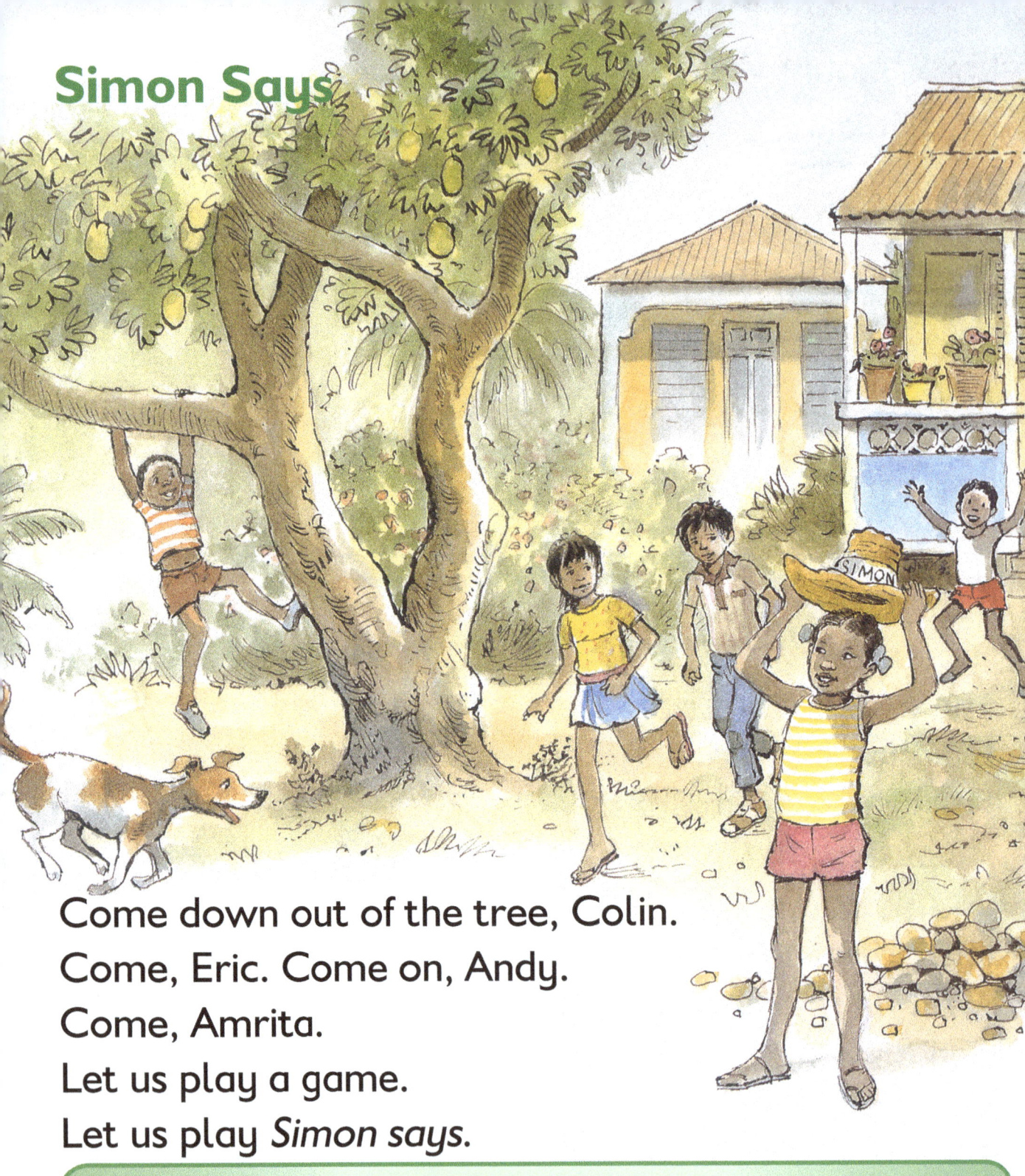

Come down out of the tree, Colin.
Come, Eric. Come on, Andy.
Come, Amrita.
Let us play a game.
Let us play *Simon says*.

PH Revise silent **e** as in **game**. Silent **e** tells you to say the name of the vowel that comes before it in the word, while the **e** remains silent. Have pupils help you make a family of words with silent **e** at the end and **a** as the first vowel, e.g., **made, fare, same**, etc. **C** What do you think Colin was doing in the tree? **LP** *Group One*: Simon says sing. *Group Two*: We are singing. *Group One*: Simon says skip. *Group Two*: We are skipping.

Simon says hop.

We are hopping.

I cannot hop.

Yes, you can, Andy. You can hop.
You must try to hop. Try, Andy.

When I try, I trip and fall.
I cannot do it, Pam.

PH Introduce **tr** sound as in **try, trip, tree**. Practise **tr** in Twister 9. Make flashcards with **tray, trunk, tree, train, truck**. Display pictures of these items in class. Have pupils match words with pictures. Revise initial **a** as in **Andy**; **h** as in **hop**; **f** as in **fall**. **C** How can you tell that Andy tried? How is the dog is feeling? How can you tell? **A** Have each pupil draw and label a tree, a train, or a truck.

17

Simon says skip. We are skipping.

I cannot skip, Pam.

You must try to skip, Andy.
You must try to play the game.

Well, I do not want to play this game.

Come on, Ruff.
We do not have to play this game.
You can play with me.
You can sit and look at me.
See, I can climb this tree, Ruff.

Simon says jump.

See, Ruff. I can jump.
I can play *Simon says*.

Where is Andy?
He is in the tree.
Do not jump, Andy.

Colin, get Mummy.
Run and get Mummy.

Do not jump, Andy!
You must not jump from the tree!

I can play the game.
I am going to jump.

No! No! No!
Andy, you must not jump from the tree.
Do not jump!

Do not jump, Andy. What are you doing in the tree?

I am playing *Simon says*, Mummy. I can jump from the tree. I can land like a jet.

Yes, you can. But you must not jump. I will help you. Let me help you.

WA Introduce word part **-ill** as in **will**. Put **f**, **p**, **m**, etc., in front to make word family. Divide class into groups. How many words can each group make? Practise Twister 11. **C** How do the children who are watching Andy feel? Do you think Andy is frightened? Give reasons for your answer. **PH** Revise **e** sound as in **let**, **help**, **get**, **jet**. Revise **j** as in **jet** and **jump**; **d** as in **do** and **down** (p. 16).

You must not jump from a tree.
You will get hurt.
You do not want to get hurt.

I do not want to get hurt, Mummy.
I want to play *Simon says*.

You can play *Simon says* with me.

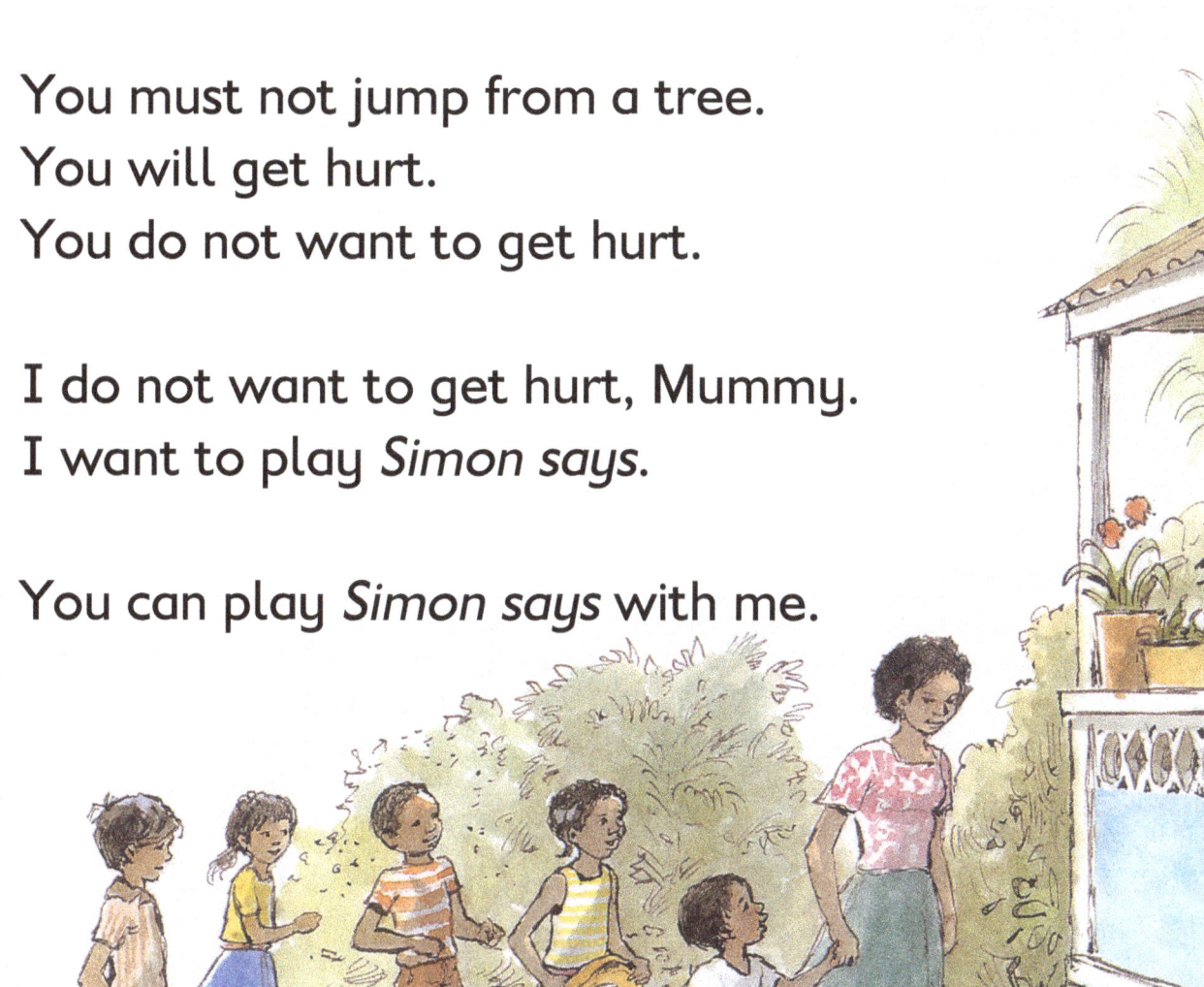

You will play with us, Mummy?

Yes. Simon says come with me.

PH Revise **pl** as in **play**; medial **u** as in **Mummy**, **jump**; **g** as in **get**. **C** Why is it bad for Andy to jump from the tree? Talk about other activities that are dangerous. Have pupils draw pictures to show things they should not do because they will get hurt. Write "Do Not" on the pictures and display them in the classroom. **C** Where is Mummy taking the children to play 'Simon Says'? Why?

We are playing *Simon says.*
Simon says sit, children. Sit and eat.

PH Revise initial **ch** as in **children** and **s** as in **sit**, **says**, and **Simon**. **C** What do you think the children in the story are eating? Talk about everyone's favourite food. Do you like the story? Have pupils make up other endings. **LP** *Teacher*: Andy hops. *Pupils*: Andy hops. *Teacher*: try *Pupils*: Andy tries. *Teacher*: skip *Pupils*: Andy skips. Use other cues such as **play, climb, look, run, eat**, etc., to drill present tense, third person singular.

What Do You Like?

Look, Eric! Look, Amrita!
Is that Uncle Roy?

Hello! Hello!
Hi, Amrita and Eric!
Come with me.
I am going to get
something you like.

Mummy and Daddy, can we go with Uncle Roy?

PH Revise **y** sound as in **you** and **yes**; **ee** in **we** and **me**; **h** as in **Hi**. **LP** *Teacher*: You and I like to go shopping. *Pupils*: You and I like to go shopping. *Teacher*: Robert and Patsy *Pupils*: Robert and Patsy like to go shopping. Use pairs of names or pronouns (**she** and **I**, **he** and **I**, etc.) to continue drilling the present tense plural forms of verbs. **C** Where do you think Uncle Roy will take the children? What do you think he will buy for them?

Where are we going?
You will see.

When will you
tell us, Uncle Roy?
Please tell us.

We are going to get
something you like.

What is it, Uncle Roy?
You will soon see.

PH Revise e sound as in **we** and **me**; point to difference between long e, as in **me** and **we**, and short e as in **Hello** (p. 25), **tell** and **get** (p. 26) Revise **pl** as in **please** and **play**. Revise i as in **like**. Remind pupils that **i** in **like** is different from **i** in **will** because of silent e. Repeat rule for silent e. Practise saying Twister 12. **C** Talk about the different shops in the picture. What does each one sell? What does the cart in the foreground sell?

What do you like?

We like toys.
There is a toy shop.
Are we going to
get toys?

No, we are going to
get something to eat.
What do you like
to eat?

PH Revise wh as in where and when (p. 26) and what (p. 27). Revise g as in going and get. LP Practise Twister 8. Teacher: I like mangoes. What do you like? 1st Pupil: I like ice cream. What do you like? Continue drill giving each pupil a turn. C How do Eric and Amrita feel? Talk about the kinds of toys, food and drink pupils like. A Pupils use question form to make poems, e.g., Where's Eric?/Gone to town./Where's Amrita?/She's gone too.

We like mangoes.
Are we going to get mangoes?

No, not mangoes.

We like bananas.
Are we going to get bananas?

No, not bananas.

C Talk about the picture. Pupils point out vendors. What does each one sell? **LP** Introduce a question and answer session, e.g., *Teacher*: What does she have for sale? *Pupil*: She has pineapples for sale. *Teacher*: What does he have for sale? *Pupil*: He has bananas for sale, etc. Let each pupil have a turn. Identify each of the vendors, so pupils answer appropriately. **PH** Revise initial **n** as in **no** and **not**. Practise Twister 13. Revise **b** as in **bananas** and **buy** (p. 29).

There is a coconut man.
We like coconuts too, Uncle Roy.
Are we going to buy coconuts from the man?

No. No. We are not buying coconuts.

Tell us where we are going, Uncle Roy.

You will see. You will soon see.

We will soon get there.

I see an ice cream shop, Uncle Roy. Are we going there?

Are we going for ice cream, Uncle Roy?
We like ice cream.
Please let us get ice cream, Uncle Roy.

PH Revise **sh** as in **shop**. Find other things in the picture that begin with **sh**, e.g., **shoes, shirt, shoulder**. Practise Twister 14. **C** Talk about whether pupils like ice cream. Which is the most popular flavour? **LP** *Teacher:* Are we going for ice cream? *Pupils:* Are we going for ice cream? *Teacher:* Coconut water. *Pupils:* Are we going for coconut water? Continue drill with names of other food items. **WA** Talk about compound word Supercones on the ICE CASTLE sign.

Yes, we are going to get ice cream.

I want mango ice cream, Uncle Roy.
I like mango ice cream.
I want coconut ice cream, Uncle Roy.
I like coconut ice-cream.
What do you want, Uncle Roy?

I want you to eat.
I like to see you eat ice cream.

C Is there anybody in your family who takes you out for treats? Who? Where do you go? Where do you like to go most of all? Why? Talk about the difference between this story and *Simon Says*. Does anything good/bad happen in this story? Does anything good/bad happen in *Simon Says*? **PH** Revise silent **e** as in **ice** and **like**. Practise Twister 12. Revise **u** as in **uncle** and **umbrella**. Revise **y** as in **yes**, **you** and Twister 4. Revise **t** sound as in **to**.

The Race

Tell us a story, Grandma.
Tell us a story.
Please tell us a story.

Grandma is going to tell us a story.

WA Make several flashcards with **-ell** and several sets of flashcards with consonants to build words like **s** + **ell**, **w** + **ell**, **b** + **ell**, etc. Which team can build most words? Practise Twister 15. **A** Does anyone know a good storyteller? Can someone tell the class a good story that he or she has recently heard? **PH** Revise **t** as in **tell**. Introduce **st** sound as in **story**. Pupils give other words that begin with **st**, e.g., **sting**, **stove**, **stamp**, **start**, **stop**.

Rabbit and Turtle are going up the road.

Rabbit says: You are slow.

Turtle says: I am not slow.

Rabbit says: You are as slow as a worm.
You cannot run a race.

Turtle says: Yes, I can. I can run a race.

Rabbit says: Run a race with me to
Mr Green's shop.

Turtle says: Okay. I will race you to his shop.

PH Revise **w** as in **worm** and **with**. Revise initial **r** as in **run**, **race**, **road**. Have pupils give other words beginning with r sound. Practise Twister 16. Use word part **-un** as in **run** to build word family, e.g., **run**, **bun**, **fun**. Revise **gr** as in **Green** and **Grandma**. **C** Why is Rabbit fast and Turtle slow? Talk about other animals in the picture. Say whether they are fast or slow.

Rabbit runs fast.
Soon he is far down the roar.
Turtle is slow. He is far behind rabbit.

Turtle is far behind.

Rabbit says: Look at me, Turtle.
You are slow.
I can run fast.
You cannot run a
race with me.

WA Introduce **behind** as a sight word. **PH** Point out **a** sound as in **fast** and **far**. Make flashcards with **-ast** and **-ar**. Use cards with **c, f, l, m, p, v** to make word family **cast, fast, last, mast, past** and **vast**. Use cards with **c, f, b** and **t** to make word family **car, far, bar, tar**. Have pupils find and say final **k** in **look**. **C** Talk about the various animals and insects in the picture. Which are fast and which are slow? Who do you think will win the race?

Rabbit is so far down the road
that he cannot see Turtle.
He is so far down the road
that he is jumping for joy.

Rabbit says: Where is Turtle? I cannot see him.
Ha! Ha! Ha!
See! I can run fast.
I am going to win this race.

PH Revise **r** sound as in **rabbit, race, road**. Revise **j** as in **jumping** and **joy**. Revise **oo** as in **look**. **C** Why is Rabbit jumping for joy? Talk about the animals in the picture. Which are fast? Which are slow? **LP** *Teacher:* I am going to win. *Pupils:* I am going to win. *Teacher:* run *Pupils:* I am going to run. *Teacher:* sleep *Pupils:* I am going to sleep. Use other action words to continue drill.

Rabbit says: Turtle is slow as a slug.
I am so far down the road
that he cannot win this race.
I am going to sleep.
See, I can sleep here.
Ha! Ha! Ha! I can sleep
and I can still win this race.

"You are quick. Yes, you can sleep."

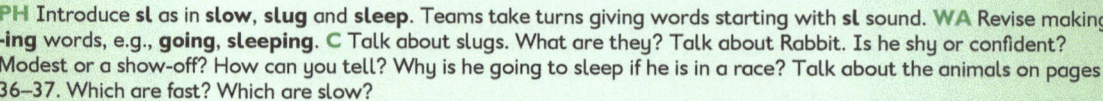

PH Introduce **sl** as in **slow**, **slug** and **sleep**. Teams take turns giving words starting with **sl** sound. **WA** Revise making **-ing** words, e.g., **going**, **sleeping**. **C** Talk about slugs. What are they? Talk about Rabbit. Is he shy or confident? Modest or a show-off? How can you tell? Why is he going to sleep if he is in a race? Talk about the animals on pages 36–37. Which are fast? Which are slow?

Turtle says: I can win this race.
Rabbit cannot see me passing him.
He is quick but now he is sleeping.
I can win this race.
I can get to Mr Green's shop first.

PH Revise **w** as in **win**. Revise **ee** as in **see** and **sleep**. Make flashcards with words and pictures for **bee**, **knee**, **tree**, **sheep**, **queen**, **seed**, **teeth**. Give pupils practice in identifying **ee** sound in these words and in Twister 17. Revise **h** as in **he**, **here** and **ha** (p. 36) and in Twister 20. Introduce **q** as in **quick**. Point out words starting with **q** in Twister 23.
C Why don't the animals wake Rabbit up? Whom do they want to win the race?

Rabbit jumps up.
He looks down the road.
He looks up the road.

Rabbit says: Where is Turtle?
He is not here.
I had a nap but I am still going to win this race.
Look at me! Ha! Ha! Ha!
I am winning!

LP *Teacher*: Rabbit jumps. *Pupils*: Rabbit jumps. *Teacher*: look *Pupils*: Rabbit looks. *Teacher*: run *Pupils*: Rabbit runs. Use other words from the story as cues to continue drill, e.g., **stop, sleep, wake, boast, lose**. Do a similar drill for Turtle, e.g., *Teacher*: Turtle crawls. *Pupils*: Turtle crawls. *Teacher*: creep *Pupils*: Turtle creeps. Continue with **try, win, laugh**.
C How long do you think Rabbit has been asleep? Where are the other animals from the previous pictures?

Rabbit can see Mr Green's shop.
He can see lots of animals.

Rabbit says: Turtle, what are you doing here? You cannot win in a race with me! You are slow. I am quick!

Turtle says: Ha! Ha! Ha! Now you see that I can win in a race with you. Ha! Ha! Ha! I win! I win!

PH Revise **ee** as in **see** and **Green**, and in **creeps**, **peeps**, etc., in Twister 17. Practise **sh** sound in Twister 14. Revise **h** as in **he** and **ha**. Revise **q** as in **quick** and in words in Twister 23. Make flashcards with **qui** and others with **-ll**, **-t**, **-ck** to make word family. Revise **sl**. **A** In teams, play a game to see who can find the most words starting with **sl**. **C** Name all the animals in the illustration. How does Rabbit feel? How does Turtle feel? Did Rabbit get what he deserved?

At the Zoo

Colin and Pam are going to the zoo.
Eric and Amrita are going to the zoo
All the boys and girls are going to the zoo.

PH Introduce **z** sound as in **zoo**. Practise Twister 18. Revise **th** as in **the**. Pupils give other words that begin with **th** as in **the**, e.g., **them, those, these, theirs, that**. **LP** Play What am I? Ask individual pupils to mime being an animal in a cage. Pupil who is acting asks: What am I? Pupils take turns to answer: You are a ... **C** Talk about zoos. Have pupils visited a zoo? Where? Which animals did they see? Which are their favourite animals? Were the animals in cages?

Pam: Hooray! We are here.
Let us go into the zoo.
Come, Andy. Stay with us.

Andy: I want to see a fox
in the zoo.
I want to
see a zebra,
too!

PH Introduce **oo** as in **zoo**, **too** and **hooray**. Make flashcards with words and pictures to show **goose**, **roof**, **broom**, **boot**, **spoon**, **moon**, **tooth**, **stool**. Revise **z** as in **zebra**; **x** as in **fox** and words ending with **x** in Twisters 2 and 6; **st** as in **stay** and words in Twister 24. **WA** Say and spell the words **stay** and **play**. Write them down. Which team can find the most words ending with **ay**? **C** Why must the children stay together?

41

Pam: Oh, look at that bird, Andy.
That bird has funny legs.
Andy! Where is Andy?
Amrita, do you see Andy?

Amrita: No, I do not see Andy.
Maybe he is looking for a fox and a zebra.

Pam: Maybe he is with the boys. Quick!
Let us see if we can find him.

LP *Teacher*: Let us look at the birds. *Pupils*: Let us look at the birds. *Teacher*: foxes *Pupils*: Let us look at the foxes. Use the names of other animals to continue the drill, e.g., **flamingos**, **turtles**, **zebras**, etc. **PH** Revise **q** as in **quick**. Practise Twister 23. Revise **z** as in **zebra**; **x** as in **fox** and in words in Twister 6. **C** Talk about the picture. Name the different birds. Can they all fly? Do you think the animal in the cage is happy? **WA** Talk about compound word **maybe**.

Pam: Here are Eric and Colin.
They are looking at the lions.
Where is Andy?
Eric, where is Andy?

Colin: He is not here, Pam.
Maybe he went to find
a fox and a zebra.

Eric: He likes snakes. Let us see
if he is looking at the snakes.

PH Revise silent **e** rule and talk about **i** in **likes**. Talk about **a** in **snake, awake, take, cake** (Twister 19). Silent **e** tells you to say the name of the letter **a**. Talk about long **e** as in **he, be** (in **maybe**) and **me**. Point out that it is the same sound as in **see, bee, tree**, etc. **A** Introduce riddles. I have four paws and a mane. I am the king of the jungle. What am I? Work in groups. Groups make up riddles and try them out on other groups.

Colin: Oh! Look at the snakes, Eric.

Amrita: I do not like snakes.
Do you like snakes, Pam?
Pam: No, I do not like snakes,
and Andy is not here.
We must try to find him.
We must look for a fox and a zebra, too.
What will we do if we do not find him?
Amrita: I will help you to look for him, Pam.

PH Revise **tr** as in **try**; final **k** as in **look**; **z** as in **zebra**; **x** as in **fox**; **c** in **Colin** and **Eric**. Introduce consonant blend **sn** as in **snake**. Ask pupils to give other **sn** words, e.g., **snail, sniff, sneeze, snore, snort**. **C** Why does Pam say, **"We must look for a fox and a zebra, too?"** Do you think Andy will find a fox? Why? Why not? How many pupils like snakes? Are all snakes dangerous? Are all dangerous snakes large? How big is the biggest snake?

Colin: Look at that cage.
Is that a monkey in that cage?
Let us look at the monkeys.

Eric: Yes, I want to see the monkeys.
Pam: I cannot look at the monkeys.
I have to find Andy. He is lost.
We must try to find him, Colin.
Colin: Let us see if he is looking at the monkeys, Pam.

PH Point out silent e in **cage**. Pupils should sound the words, saying the name of the letter **a**. Revise Twister 19. Revise **m** as in **monkey**; **l** as in **look, let, lost**. **C** Discuss all the cages you can see and the animals inside them. Talk about why the cages are different. Do you think animals like being in cages? Talk about the shape, colour, size and personality of the animals. Look closely at the picture to see if you can find Andy. Do you think Pam is a responsible girl? Why?

Colin: Here is Andy. He is not lost.
Andy: No, I am not lost. I am sad. This man says there is no fox or zebra in the zoo.

LP *Teacher:* Here is the ostrich. *Pupils:* Here is the ostrich. *Teacher:* monkey *Pupils:* Here is the monkey. *Teacher:* snake *Pupils:* Here is the snake. Continue drill, using names of other animals. **C** Look at people's faces on both pages. Try to imagine what each one is thinking or saying. Do you think Colin is a responsible boy? Why? **PH** Revise **z** as in **zoo** and **zebra**; **h** as in **here**, **he**, and **helping**, and in Twister 20; **m** as in **man**, etc.

Pam: What are you doing here, Andy?
Andy: I am helping the man to feed the monkeys.
Man: Yes, he is helping me. He is a kind boy.

PH Revise **k** as in **kind**; **x** as in **fox** (p. 46) and **f** as in **fox** and **feed**. **LP** Use drill on page 46 in the plural form, e.g., *Teacher:* Here are the monkeys. *Pupils:* Here are the monkeys. *Teacher:* foxes *Pupils:* Here are the foxes. **A** Each pupil pretends to be an animal and answers the question "What do you eat?" in a complete sentence. **C** Imagine you are one of the animals in the picture. Tell the class what you are thinking as you look out at the visitors.

Eric: I want to see the lions again.
Amrita: I want to see the birds again.
Colin: I want to see the snakes again.
Andy: I still want to see a fox and a zebra.
Pam: Stay with us, Andy. You must not get lost.
Andy: I was not lost but I will stay with you.

PH Revise **ee** sound as in **seed** and **feed**; **oo** as in **zoo**, **soon**, **hooray**; **z** as in **zoo** and **zebra**; **ch** as in **cheer** and **children**; **st** as in **stay** and **lost**. Have pupils give other words ending with **st**, e.g., **post**, **fast**. **C** Did the children enjoy themselves? Do you think Andy was lost? **A** Let pupils talk about whether cages are the best way to keep animals in a zoo. Have pupils make a model zoo with boxes, paints, crayons. Make animals from papier maché, or cut them out.